YOUR KNOWLEDGE HAS VALUE

Bibliographic information published by the German National Library:

The German National Library lists this publication in the National Bibliography; detailed bibliographic data are available on the Internet at http://dnb.dnb.de .

Imprint:

Copyright © 2009 GRIN Verlag, Open Publishing GmbH
Print and binding: Books on Demand GmbH, Norderstedt Germany
ISBN: 9783640618743

This book at GRIN:

http://www.grin.com/en/e-book/150603/bill-gates-change-agent-of-information-technology

Kayla Murdock

Bill Gates - Change Agent of Information Technology

A Short Biography

GRIN Publishing

GRIN - Your knowledge has value

Since its foundation in 1998, GRIN has specialized in publishing academic texts by students, college teachers and other academics as e-book and printed book. The website www.grin.com is an ideal platform for presenting term papers, final papers, scientific essays, dissertations and specialist books.

Visit us on the internet:

http://www.grin.com/

http://www.facebook.com/grincom

http://www.twitter.com/grin_com

Bill Gates – Change Agent of Information Technology

Spring 2010

In a Microsoft Information Technology interview in 1997, Bill Gates said that "Software is a big change agent in the world today…" (Gates, 1997). While I agree with his philosophy of software in the world today, Gates humbly failed to mention that he is the reason software has become such an enhancing instrument in today's society. William (Bill) Gates III, is known as one of the richest entrepreneurs in the world, and doesn't even hold a college degree. He is one of the most influential people in the world. Gates took a leap in faith by dropping out of Harvard his junior year to chase his dream. He didn't know that his creation would change the world's information technology forever, yet he still took a blind leap of faith and technology has soared because of it. Bill Gates took his power and financial success and became an immense philanthropist that has helped boost many charities and foundations today (Coley, 2009). For these, and an additional endless list of explanations, Bill Gates should be considered the most powerful change agent of the century for information technology.

"I'm a great believer that any tool that enhances communication has profound effects in terms of how people can learn from each other, and how they can achieve the kind of freedoms that they're interested in" (BrainyMedia, 2010). One of the enhancing tools that Bill Gates was discussing was his creation, Microsoft. Microsoft was created by Gates and his partner Paul Allen in 1975, and revolutionized the computer industry from that day forward. Microsoft helped to formulate the computer easier to use with its developed and purchased software, and made it a commercial success. Gates and Allen were directed by a belief that the personal computer would be an important instrument on every office desktop and in every home. Gates' foresight and vision as regards to personal computing have been central to the achievement of Microsoft and the software industry. In 1980, the company inked a landmark deal with IBM to produce an operating system for its up-and-coming personal computer (PC). Microsoft bought 86-DOS from Seattle Computer Products, a Disk Operating System designed for 8086-based computers. It used the 86-DOS code as the basis for IBM's first PC Operating System, which became known as PC-DOS. When clones of IBM's PC started to appear, Microsoft pushed their own version of PC-DOS, MS-DOS, to system builders (Bellis, 2009).

Gates is enthusiastically involved in key management and tactical decisions at Microsoft, and plays an important role in the technical development of new products.

Much of his time is dedicated to meeting with customers and staying in contact with Microsoft employees around the world through e-mail. Under Gates' guidance, Microsoft's mission is continuously to advance and progress software technology, and to make it easier, more cost-effective and more enjoyable for people to use computers. Microsoft Research invests for the long run, with projects typically running three to nine years to commercialization. The company is dedicated to a long-term vision, which is reflected in its investment of some $6.8 billion for research and development during the current fiscal year (Bender, 2004).

Among Microsoft's many achievements were MS-DOS, Word, Excel, Macintosh software and Windows. The company relied on the success of Windows, banking every penny they had on its success, which paid off in Microsoft's second phase from 1990, when Windows 3.0 was released, to 1994. Customer driven change also marked phase two. Customers wanted operating systems that blended the best of Windows, UNIX, and NetWare, this was the beginning of Windows NT. Customers wanted the finest of Microsoft's productivity tools to work better together, so Microsoft Office was created to integrate the software. Recognizing the need to expand fundamental advances in software, Microsoft created Microsoft Research. In 1995 Microsoft entered phase three, taking advantage of tremendous opportunities offered by the Internet. Since 1995 Microsoft has reinvented itself so that, today, everything Microsoft creates or updates leverages with the Internet. In the beginning Gates' was mainly concerned and involved with technical development of new products in order to attract consumers. Since Microsoft controls the largest percentage of the market than any of its competitors Gates' puts more focus on the organization itself and its employees (Bellis, 2009).

Microsoft's mission is to continually advance and improve software technology and to make it easier, more cost effective and more enjoyable for people to use computers. In order for Microsoft to continue on its fruitful path the development of intelligent decision makers, otherwise known as managers, must be trained. Gates' realizes the ROI of his formation relies on every single individual, which makes up the organization called Microsoft. He also knows he cannot be at the table to make ever single day-to-day decision, instead of trying to be in a hundred places at once Gates' attempts to train well oiled managers. He has even published articles that reveal his expectations and qualities he attempts to instill into Microsoft managers. Gates' believes in talking with employees and customers rather than talking at them. By conducting conversations individuals, especially customers, can understand and allow them to provide feedback that is taken into consideration allows Gates' to build a lasting and trusting relationship with employees and customers. Gates used the charismatic, transactional, and the transformational styles. While utilizing his charismatic style, Bill Gates used ethics, morals, self-confidence, enthusiasm, and a passion for creating an empire as well as inspiring his subordinates. (Bellis, 2009).

It is important to understand what Gates' invention of Microsoft software has done for society, to understand why Bill Gates should be considered one of the greatest change agents of information technology. Today, Microsoft software is everywhere and undeniably is almost synonymous with the terms "computer" and "Internet". Bill Gates innovation brought popularity to computers, and showed not only individuals but also organizations what they have been missing without it. Individuals benefited from the access to the computer and Microsoft by using Microsoft Word as a communication wave length between students and teachers, and peers. Meanwhile, families use tools from Microsoft Office such as Excel for family budgeting, Outlook to connect with their relatives, and the many other tools for entertainment purposes. Microsoft Windows is one of the most commonly used operation systems that is user friendly and satisfies most of Microsoft's millions of customers. From the beginning, Gates said that customers who are upset are the best learning tools for a company (Gates, 1997). Since its invention, Microsoft has controlled a major portion of the computer industry. While Microsoft did not invent the very first word processor, they have invented the world's most successful one. People today know that Windows and Office go hand-in-hand and the latest iterations of the program blow other alternatives like Open Office out of the water.

Microsoft managed to really market their word processor after 1984 when Macs with true GUIs and then-sophisticated processors could finally handle a 'what you see is what you get' program. Today, Microsoft's Office program is a game-changer, and one of the company's largest selling divisions after the Windows OS. The Office word processor has become much more than simply Microsoft's Word, which is the main word processor. Everything from PowerPoint to Excel to Outlook to Publisher have changed the way we think about editing and viewing documents and presentations on a computer (Ziberg, 2008).

He created the famous mission statement for Microsoft, to put "a computer on every desk and in every home." However, homes aren't the only place where Microsoft thrives. Business' picked up on Microsoft and ran with it, using the office suite and operating system to help build and run successful companies. Every day, millions of people in the business world are typing letters on Microsoft Word, figuring data on Microsoft Excel, and giving presentations with Microsoft PowerPoint. National and international business is conducted by the simple email program Microsoft Outlook. Microsoft has improved productivity, communication, innovation, and research and development in the workplace today. It is amazing how Bill Gates' innovation has changed the way hundreds of countries do business today. When you look back at the career of Bill Gates, it's easy to focus on Microsoft's biggest product – Windows. It powers business servers, mobile phones, PDAs, cash machines, retail displays, set-top boxes and old Sega Dreamcast consoles. Windows is everywhere. Windows 95 was arguably the game-changer (Cooley, 2009).

Imagine trying to do a presentation without PowerPoint to back you up. Imagine having to write a paper without the use of Microsoft Word. Imagine trying to quickly calculate a budget without using Microsoft Excel. Simply put, while there have been imitators and competitors; Microsoft's Office is so successful that they even ported a version over to the Mac OSX as a result of consumer demand. Much more important than the Office Suite of programs, is the Windows OS in terms of everything from Microsoft's revenue to cultural impact. Apple was the first company to make a commercially viable PC, but it wasn't until Windows that the PC finally entered the public imagination. Apple's case was similar to the one with the Betamax in the 1980's losing the fight to the VHS. Simply put, you could install a Windows OS on anything that had IBM architecture to it. Soon after the advent of the Windows OS, the PC was quickly on its way to becoming a household term. There were many ups and downs for Microsoft and Bill Gates, and many argue that they lost their touch when Windows ME was released. Now, Windows 7 looks to rightfully regain the throne that they established back in 1995. Everything from the taskbar to the start menu to the Windows

Explorer has become a part of common knowledge because of smart marketing by Microsoft (Ziberg, 2008).

Bill Gates stepped down from the Chief Executive Officer position of Microsoft in June 2008. He remained as chairman and created the position of chief software architect. Gates announced that he would be transitioning from full-time work at Microsoft to part-time work, and work full-time as a philanthropist at the Bill & Melinda Gates Foundation. He gradually transferred his duties to Ray Ozzie and Craig Mundie, chief research and strategy officer. He remains at Microsoft as non-executive chairman. Microsoft without its full-time founder is still fairing well, even with Gates only popping in as a part-timer. Its cash cows, Windows and Office, still earn huge sums and there are new enterprises such as Xbox and Windows Server, IT in the heart of businesses that are substantial and growing. After he left Microsoft, his number one goal was giving away his money by promoting research into neglected diseases and finding other ways to improve the lives of the poor of the world (Miller, 2008). Bill Gates accomplished his mission statement, and felt that it was time for him to move on to help the world with another tool – his money. This is just one of the many reasons why Bill Gates should be recognized as one of the most influential leaders of our time.

In addition to his enthusiasm for computers, Gates is fascinated in biotechnology. He sits on the board of the ICOS Corporation and is a shareholder in Chiroscience Group of the United Kingdom and its wholly owned subsidiary, Chiroscience Research and Development Inc. (formerly Darwin Molecular) of Bothell, Wash. Gates also founded Corbis Corporation, which is building one of the largest resources of visual information in the world - a wide-ranging digital collection of art and photography from public and private collections around the globe. Gates also has invested with cellular telephone pioneer Craig McCaw in Teledesic, a company that is working on an ambitious plan to launch hundreds of low-orbit satellites around the Earth to provide a worldwide two-way broadband telecommunications service (Jooste, 2009).

Between the Bill Gates scholarships for minorities and the Bill and Melinda Gates Foundation, his philanthropy is going beyond just mere 'helping'. Bill Gates wealth has globally enhanced health care, reduced extreme poverty, expanded education opportunities and access to information technology. According to a 2004 Forbes magazine article, Gates gave away over $29 billion to charities since 2000 (Forbes, 2004). Bill Gates philanthropy has been used in AIDS prevention and other diseases prevalent in third world countries. The Bill and Melinda Gates Foundation claims to be the world's biggest philanthropic organization, and none have yet stepped forward to contradict that.

According to Bill Gates 2010 Annual letter for the Bill and Melinda Gates Foundation, he says that the most important way to give back is to innovate ways to improve the way of life. Not only for our economy, but for the third world countries who need improvements in health and their economic ways. He discusses the need for vaccines, online learning, helping teachers improve, generosity, and the need for cures to many illnesses (Gates, 2010). Judging by his letter alone, you can tell that he cares. He understands that being one of the richest men in the world, he can make a difference.

Bill Gates might be best known as the co-founder of Microsoft and the world's richest man, but there's a much more to the Microsoft chairman that the world is getting to know. For years, Gates has been a philanthropist, giving money through his Bill & Melinda Gates Foundation. But in recent months, Gates has been more vocal; using his power to share his opinion on helping people around the globe, as well as policies that he believes could improve the economy. As much as that has helped people, it has also helped Microsoft. When Gates left day-to-day operations at Microsoft a few years ago to pursue his philanthropic efforts, some wondered how his reduced presence would affect the software giant.

Bill Gates not only knows how to build a successful software platform, he also understands the underlying issues that will make or break a particular endeavor. That's especially important when one considers his philanthropic efforts. Gates understands the issues surrounding a problem and sets out to find a solution. That's precisely why his Bill & Melinda Gates Foundation have been so successful in bringing better health to people in countries around the world. Unlike so many other software companies that came before and after, Microsoft was able to build a lasting empire. Windows, Office and Internet Explorer have entered the vast majority of homes across the world. But by understanding business, Gates is also able to effect change. He can be relied upon to offer solutions to our current economic crisis. Perhaps that's why he has been so vocal lately about the best course of action in bringing jobs back to the United States.

In conclusion, it is difficult to sum up one particular reason as to why Bill Gates should be considered one of the most influential, well known change agents of his time. Whether it is for co-founding Microsoft to his outstanding philanthropist generosity, Bill Gates has changed the way that the world looks at information technology. To those who say the computer revolution would have happened without him, he can point out that more than 90% of computers run Microsoft's Windows (Miller, 2008). He has also changed the way people should view the wealthy. He has given up most of his control over Microsoft to pursue his mission of philanthropy and giving back to his customers and the world.

Bibliography

Bellis, M. (2009). *The Unusual History of Microsoft Windows*. Retrieved January 30,
    2010, from http://inventors.about.com/od/mstartinventions/a/Windows.htm

Bender, E. (2004, February 27). *The Ultimate Change Agent*. Retrieved January 30,
    2010, from http://www.technologyreview.com/computing/13469/?a=f.

BrainyMedia. (2010). *Bill Gate's quotes*. Retrieved January 30, 2010, from
    http://www.brainyquote.com/quotes/authors/b/bill_gates.html.

Coley, A. (2009, January 1). *Historical Examples of Courage: (No.13) Bill Gates
    Quotations About Perseverance, Patience and Education*. Retrieved January 30,
    2010, from
    http://www.associatedcontent.com/article/1354311/historical_examples_of_courag
    e_no13.html?cat=9

Forbes Magazine. (2004). *Forbes World's Richest People 2004 - Bill Gates*.
    Retrieved January 30, 2010, from
    http://www.forbes.com/finance/lists/10/2004/LIR.jhtml?passListId=10&passYear
    =2004&passListType=Person&uniqueId=BH69&datatype=Person.

Gates, B. (1997). *Bill Gates will lead Microsoft into his 50's*. Windows IT Pro.
Retrieved
    January 30, 2010, from http://windowsitpro.com/article/articleid/16941/bill-gates-
    will-lead-microsoft-into-his-50s.html.

Gates, B. (2010). *2010 Annual Letter from Bill gates*. Retrieved January 30, 2010, from
    http://www.gatesfoundation.org/annual-letter/2010/Pages/annual-letter-
conclusion.aspx.

Jooste, R. (2009, October 20). *Companies that changed our world as we know it*.
    Retrieved January 30, 2010, from http://www.gitui.com/internet/companies-that-
    changed-our-world-as-we-know-it/.

Miller, C. (2008, June 19). *Bill Gates: How a geek changed the world*. Retrieved
January 30,
    2010, from http://news.bbc.co.uk/2/hi/7461783.stm.

Ziberg, C. (2008, June 26). *Bill Gates Milestones*. Retrieved January 30, 2010, from \
    http://www.tomsguide.com/us/Bill-Gates,news-1787.html.